DID YOU CHOOSE THE RIGHT PATH?

DID YOU CHOOSE THE RIGHT PATH?

GR8 RELATIONSHIPS

EQUIP PRESS

Colorado Springs

DID YOU CHOOSE THE RIGHT PATH?

First Edition: 2023
Did You Choose the Right Path? / (GR8 Relationships)
Paperback ISBN: : 978-1-958585-43-6
eBook ISBN: 978-1-958585-44-3

EQUIP PRESS
Colorado Springs

CONTENTS

INTRODUCTION

Choosing the right path in life impacts all you do. At GR8 Relationships, the basic premise of choosing the right path has to do with who you serve. Do you serve yourself, your wants and needs, or do you take the path to serve and glorify God?

When you choose the path to glorify God, you also choose the path of serving and loving others because that is what God does for you. This path also leads to healthy and long-lasting relationships. When you desire the best for someone else, you will be fulfilled. This desire takes intentional focus: observing your own behavior to determine whether you are really focusing on serving and trusting God or focusing on serving your own needs and trusting in yourself. You might even be *doing* a lot for God, like teaching Bible study, serving as a deacon, and managing the pancake supper to raise money for the new baseball field at church, but are you serving Him and trusting Him?

In marriages, when people focus on God first, it's amazing to see how that primary relationship strengthens the relationship between a man and a woman. God has designed man and woman so that they can both serve and glorify God *and* do what's best for the other person. This applies to any other important relationship you have as well. In business, if you have a business partner, when you both want the highest and best for the other person, you both win. You will both be focused on making the business prosper. Let's say you are doing volunteer work on a team for a non-profit. Obviously, when the volunteer team is focused on the highest and best for the non-profit, it will prosper. Additionally, if team members are focused on serving others in the work for the non-profit, everyone wins. This prevents people from focusing on selfish gains by working for the non-profit.

Focusing on the highest and best for others requires a commitment to Godly thinking because we naturally gravitate toward meeting our needs. When you trust God, you don't work so hard to make yourself look good. When everything you do is focused on glorying Him rather than pleasing the world or yourself, your heart and spirit will be lifted to a place of deep joy and accomplishment.

Here are two verses from Isaiah:

> *If you extend your soul to the hungry*
> *And satisfy the afflicted soul,*
> *Then your light shall dawn in the darkness,*
> *And your darkness shall be as the noonday.*
> *The LORD will guide you continually,*

And satisfy your soul in drought,
And strengthen your bones;
You shall be like a watered garden,
And like a spring of water,
whose waters do not fail.

Isaiah 58:10–11, NKJV

It may not be obvious, but the first two lines are about serving others. Then notice that the remainder is about what God does for you! Doing what God asks is so much more satisfying than constantly focusing on getting your own needs met and making yourself the center of attention.

This book will explore the two paths you can take in life based on your fundamental choice of trusting God or trusting something other than God. It sounds simple, and it is. One simple, deliberate choice to glorify God. That consistent choice benefits you with the power of the life of Christ in you and the energy of the Holy Spirit working through you to overcome your sin nature and serve Him.

It is just like Isaiah 58:10-11 and many other verses tell you: choose God's way, trust in His *perfection* and believe that His ways work, and He will gladly energize and bless you with the transcendent values of love, joy, peace, patience, kindness, goodness, faithfulness, gentleness, and self-control.

Satan wants you to think that trusting God, walking in His ways, and serving others is hard because the thoughts of the sin nature never trust God. If you allow Satan to keep that thought in your mind, you miss the power of God working through you. Walking with God is not based on your strength, resolution, or energy. It is about faith in His desire to transform you into the image of Christ as you choose to trust and let Him live through you.

GLORIFY GOD OR SELF

As you, a child of God, walk through life, you constantly face two options: self or God. You can focus on glorifying yourself to get your needs met, or you can focus on God, glorify Him, and trust Him to meet your needs. When you focus on glorifying God, guess what, because you become like Him, you focus on what is best for others. The path you follow demonstrates who you trust. Do you trust God or something or someone other than God?

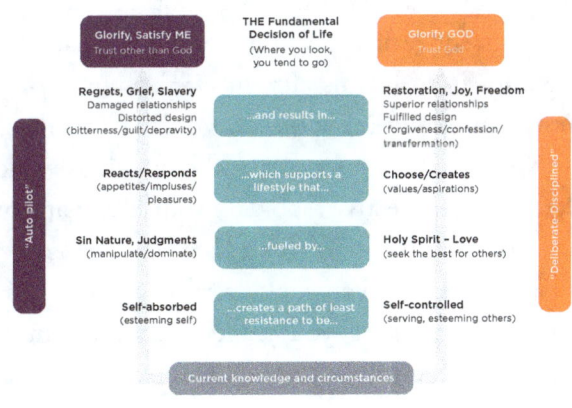

Look at the chart above. Notice the steps in the path on the left.

The path or action you take depends on where you look or place your focus. Because of sin, your natural disposition is to focus on yourself. But if you as a believer trust the Spirit of the Most-High God who dwells within you, your focus can shift from *ME* to glorifying God, which is the ultimate aim for life.

You are designed in the image of God. You only need to depend upon God to allow your design to reflect the image of God. However, your natural tendency is to depend on yourself, which will hide or distort your design. Your auto-pilot to depend on and trust *ME* follows the Self-absorbed and Judgment path on the left. You must make a deliberate choice to trust God and follow the path on the right.

When you look at your Current Reality, which is comprised of knowledge and circumstances, some things are known, and others are not. A critical part of your current reality is you either know what God is asking you to do in this current circumstance, or you do not. You either know God's Word, or you do not. God's Word is all about *reality* and how things work. If you created an objective report on your life, that would be a reasonable picture of your *Current Knowledge and Circumstances* or as you have learned – your current reality. That is where you stand right now, in that current knowledge and circumstances rectangle.

As you stand at the base of the above graphic, you have two clear choices or places to look, and paths to follow. Remember, *where you look, you tend to go.* God asks you where you are looking when He asks the fundamental question, "Do you trust God or something other than God?"

That is your fundamental decision in life. God continually asks you that one question. It comes in two critical forms, one for your eternal life, "Do you trust Me for your eternity?" and for your daily life, "Do you trust Me now?"

If you have accepted the gift of Salvation, eternal life with God, you will now be asked the second question. If you have not accepted God's gift, you will be getting the first question, and often the second question to drive you back to the first one. We all face these two questions. If you are blind to them, then you absolutely are depending on yourself, not God. Looking at God and trusting Him provides the best results.

If you look at *Satisfy ME* or *Trust something other than God,* that creates a path of least resistance to being self-absorbed and self-dependent. That is the natural tendency of the sin nature to esteem yourself rather than others. When temptation comes, you have a greater chance to sin because of your self-absorbed, satisfy ME attitude. You will be less willing to endure short-term pain; therefore, you will experience long-term pain from the regrets of your self-absorbed actions. On the other hand, if you look at *Glorify and Trust God*, He provides the energy of the Holy Spirit and His fruit of self-control. He will provide the strength to endure pain and reap eternal rewards and results. That helps you see temptation for what it is, the slippery slope to sin.

Here's what the Apostle Paul says to the Corinthians,

> *No temptation has overtaken you except such as is common to man; but God is faithful, who will not allow you to be tempted beyond what you are able, but with the temptation will also make the way of escape, that you may be able to bear it.*

1 Corinthians 10:13

Temptation is always an opportunity to operate in life without input from God or godly sources. Temptation is not the sin. Sin means succumbing to the temptation, following what the temptation is prompting you to do. The only effective way to handle temptation is to trust God and His power, not your own.

If you have started up the *Satisfy ME* path, the judgments provide more fuel for the self-absorbed focus. These judgments fuel a desire in a woman to make her relationships meet her needs and fuel the desire in a man for work and activities to meet his needs. Women will act in ways to remove pain in relationships, but will end up manipulating or dominating the relationship and creating more pain. Men, on the other hand, will act in ways to remove pain in work and will try to control work and activities and *rule* his wife, but will be left with pain both at work and home. Both men and women will focus on controlling to get their needs met. But the other path of trusting God means a completely different approach and attitude. It is not about *ME*. It is about others; therefore, actions and life are fueled by the Holy Spirit and His fruit of Love—pursuing the best for others, patiently, kindly, sacrificially, and unconditionally.

On the *Satisfy ME* path the situation gets worse. The Judgments fuel self-absorbed tendencies and further support a react/respond lifestyle focused on short term appetites, impulses, and pleasures. This lifestyle leads to statements like, "you made me mad," "I'm tired of you doing that," or "I'm getting a divorce, because she/he did . . . " This lifestyle is contrasted against a life that depends on God. Fueled by the Holy Spirit, lives become about choosing or creating. Choosing Godly values and aspirations creates a life that chooses to align our thinking with God's thinking, which changes our feelings and actions. Good thinking drives right feelings and actions. Bad thinking drives poor and rationalized feelings and actions.

Depending on which path you choose, you will encounter drastically different results. Depending upon yourself leads to Regrets, Grief and Slavery and the cycle continues with short periods of less grief, which masquerade as Peace and Joy. On the other hand, if you depend on God—desire to *Trust God*, you will have a life driven from the inside out, not the outside in like the react/respond life. The end result is Restoration, Renewal, and Freedom in spite of the people or circumstances around you. You will be solidly focused on God, who is in control of life, who alone can make sense out of life for you.

So, which path are you on? Trusting self—leading to regrets, grief, and slavery? Or, trusting God—leading to restoration, renewal, and freedom? All it requires is one fundamental choice.

> *And do not present your members as instruments of unrighteousness to sin but present yourselves to God as being alive from the dead, and your members as instruments of righteousness to God.*

> **Romans 6:13, NKJV**

Will you trust and depend on God, serving others with your design, glorifying God, and reflecting God's Image? Or will you trust yourself, serving and trying to satisfy *ME* using or distorting your design, and distort God's image? Will you walk in the Spirit, or in the Flesh?

Which path will you choose today? Your eternity, daily thoughts, feelings, actions and, especially the health of any relationship can be boiled down to this fundamental choice.

God designed us and it is only God who knows what is best for us. Following a path to glorifying God will lead us to desirable results and a life that is filled with the leading of the Holy Spirit, Who creates and restores us to superior and rewarding relationships.

Life Questions — Two Ways to Live

The best way to determine the path you are on (glorifying yourself or God) is self-examination. You may even feel that you are on fire for God and leading a life based on glorifying Him but not realize you are not always on track. The scenario below will give you some insight into the difference between living for yourself or living to glorify God. Read it and answer the questions that follow.

Which Path Are They On?

Mary and George have been married for 20 years and have struggled in their marriage primarily over how to raise the kids and managing finances. Mary is 45 and works from home as a bookkeeper. She uses her earnings to make contributions to the children's college fund. George is 52 and works as a regional manager for a large retailer.

Mary and George have four children. Jason is 18 and just finishing high school. He is not planning to go to college because he has an entrepreneurial bug and wants to try his hand at running his own home-based business. Aaron is 17 and hoping to enter a four-year university to study Math. He does not have the grades to receive a scholarship, so Mary knows they will have to fund his college through financial aid, her income and what Aaron can make as a working student. Tiffany is 15 and very active in High School, she is a majorette for the marching band, a member of the student council and president of the Anchor Club, which serves underprivileged communities. Tiffany is also very active in the youth group at their church. Stephanie is 10 and mostly interested in hanging out with her mom. She is very quiet, likes to read and help her mom cook the family meals each night.

Mary gave up a career as an accountant when the children were born. She has accepted her role as a support to her husband and to manage the household. George has had difficulty making enough money to support four kids and his wife, so Mary was glad to pitch in to make the finances work by working from home as a bookkeeper.

Because George has had difficulty supporting the family, he has developed an attitude that is self-sufficient. He feels like he must provide for the family, and that he is the only one who can make enough money to support the family. As a result of this he has become controlling and manipulative of Mary and the kids. On top of that, to validate himself, he works long and late hours most days.

Mary and George's arguments center on her going back to full-time work. She feels like that would be the best option to relieve the financial stress on the family, but George is adamant that she stays home. George says that Mary is too lax and laid back in how she relates to the kids, that they are undisciplined due to this. Mary feels like George is too rigid with rules and that this stresses out the children. They are afraid to relate to him because he is so focused on the kids being perfect in everything.

They went to see Pastor James Abimbola at church to talk through their differences. Here's how the conversation went.

George starts the conversation by saying, "Pastor James, thank you for meeting with us. We know how busy you are."

Mary nods in agreement.

Pastor James responds, "I'm always happy to meet with people who want to work things through. Too many people just don't communicate honestly with each other and that leads to problems."

George and Mary nod in agreement.

Pastor James asks, "Mary, on the phone you said that you and George do not agree on whether you should go get a full-time job or not. George, would you agree with that?"

"Well, I don't really see it that way. I think we are having disagreements about how the house is managed. If Mary goes back to work full-time, I'm afraid our house would fall apart."

Mary feels her heart-rate racing and her face turning flush because she feels this is an underhanded criticism, indicating that she can't manage a full-time job and keeping the house in order. Her mind wanders to George not being around to help with household chores and raising the kids. But she decides not to create a stir and sits in silence.

Pastor James, noticing her obvious silence asks, "Mary, do you have something to add or a different viewpoint?"

"I'll just say, I'm pretty confident that I can manage work and home. I'm pretty good at multi-tasking and my accounting background certainly helps in terms of handling finances, which we need to get in order. I can get help to manage the house. Plenty of people who need work can clean houses, do yardwork and even shuttle kids to soccer, play or choir practice."

Pastor James looks at George to see his reaction.

George sits in silence, feeling some shame that his job doesn't allow Mary to stay home with no financial consequences. He thinks to himself, "Well, I can get a second job if I have to! This is my responsibility. God created me to work and provide. I'm going to make it happen no matter what Mary says."

The session continues for a few more minutes with some awkward silence from all three people. Pastor James realizes he has uncovered some hidden issues that he cannot make Mary and George talk about in the session, so he changes the focus a bit.

"This may not seem related," he says, "but Mary, tell me about your relationship with God."

She looks at him quizzically and says, "Well, I pray. I ask God to take care of our finances. But, you know, He doesn't know how to operate an Excel spreadsheet. I have to rely on my education and experience to manage our finances the best I can."

Pastor James nods, recognizing that Mary is self-dependent and not necessarily dependent on God or focusing on building a relationship with Him, even though she prays.

"So, Mary, would you say your life is focused on glorifying God for His ultimate joy in your life?"

Again, Mary looks at the Pastor as though he is speaking a foreign language. "You know Pastor, I'm so busy doing my part-time job, running the kids around, managing the household, that I don't really have time to think about joy in my life. I'm just trying to get everything done on our limited budget. I'm not sure God really cares about that. Someday, they will all be grown, then I can take a really long vacation."

Pastor James realizes that Mary probably doesn't know she can choose a path of glorifying God for fulfillment in her life, so he decides to table that line of discovery for a different discussion.

He smiles at Mary and says, "Well, it's a vacation you will deserve."

George says, "Pastor, what do you mean about living with God's ultimate joy in our lives? I just work,

work, work and don't seem to get anywhere. My dad always provided for us, and I was raised knowing it's my responsibility to provide for the family. So that's what I'm focused on. We go to church and bring the kids along, but I don't really think of God so much during the work week."

Pastor James looks kindly at George and Mary and says, "You know, we get so busy with *doing* instead of *being* in a relationship with God that our focus in life can get off-kilter. I'm leading a couple's class on Sunday mornings where we focus on how to make God our first focus rather than our need to take control of things. I'd love for you to join us Sunday. Also, after you attend the class, we can continue the topics we've discussed today. In the meantime, I suggest that you and Mary spend some time together praying and thinking about God, asking Him to direct you. Feel free to call or email me any time if I can help."

Mary and George left the meeting with new ideas around life focus. Both of them thought to themselves that it never occurred to them to spend their lives glorifying God, or even focusing on a relationship with Him. Both of them felt good about the meeting with the pastor, even though they didn't totally understand what he was talking about.

REFLECTIVE QUESTIONS

Based on the scenario above, answer the questions below regarding which path Mary and George are on.

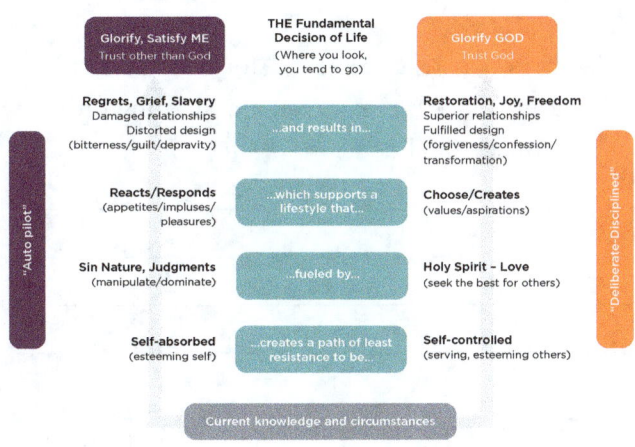

- What path are Mary and George on? What behaviors indicate that? Relate their behaviors to the steps in the path.

_____

_____

_____

_____

- How could they change what they are doing to improve their path?

_____

_____

_____

_____

- What do you relate to in the story? What does it indicate about the path you are traveling on in the fundamental decisions of life?

_____

_____

_____

_____

- What do you need to change? What do you need to continue doing?

_____

_____

_____

_____

Life Questions

The questions below will help you determine which path you are taking in your life. Spend some time reflecting on these.

- Will I be in Heaven for sure when I die? How can I be sure?
- Will I depend on God or something or someone else?
- Will I seek a relationship with Jesus Christ first, before relating to others?
- Will I operate in my design and be who God made me to be?
- Will I accept others for who they are and value them?
- Will I pursue the best for others or primarily myself?
- Will I make life about me or about others?
- Will I make decisions and act based on faith and truth or fear?
- Will I organize my life around what really matters?
- Will I spend my life trying to get others to change or focus on changing me?
- Will I use the past for learning or for control and manipulation?
- Will I live primarily in the past, present or future?

- Will I operate my life in freedom, non-judgmental and stand for truth?
- Will I make choices based on reality or on concepts, theories, and opinions?
- Will I focus on aspirations and values or will I look for immediate, short term gratification?
- Will I stand on good values or will I be a people pleaser?
- Will I look for and act upon what is right, or will I look for what's wrong?
- Will I use each situation as a catalyst to grow or to blame others and/or beat myself up?
- Will I focus more energy on using and enhancing my strengths and the strengths of others or will I focus on weaknesses?

Based on your answers to these questions, do you feel you are focused on God, or yourself?

Who Will You Serve?

What or who do you choose to serve? Based on the graph above, are you trying to glorify yourself, or glorify God? Those can be hard questions to answer, especially if you have never thought about them before. Let's put this is the context of the Path of Least Resistance for Men and Women based on their designs.

There, Here, and Path (THP)

The below graphs illustrate the best Path for Women and Men, which is to Glorify God using their Godly designs. THP charts demonstrate a natural way your mind works for creating or problem-solving.

When creating, start with a clear THERE. Next, identify where you are: HERE. Finally, develop your

PATH to move from HERE to THERE. If you are problem-solving, start with a clear HERE. Next, identify where you want to go (THERE) and develop your PATH of actions. Each process requires clarity of THERE and HERE before you start developing any actions on the PATH.

Woman's Design – Path of Least Resistance

A THP chart is helpful when talking about the design of men and women. If a woman wants to fulfill her design, she focuses on how God designed her (Genesis 2:21-23, Titus 2:1-8, Ephesians 5:22, etc.). In the THP graphic, she could write those scripture passages into the

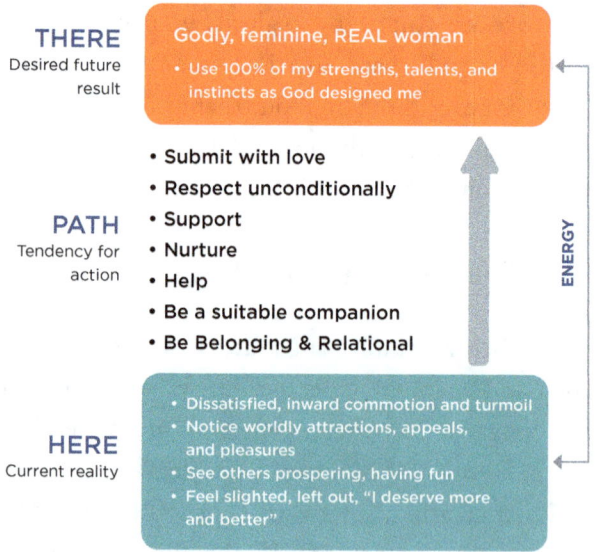

THERE rectangle to represent what she wants to accomplish. The HERE rectangle could be changed to describe her current reality and circumstances. Then she could use the seven items listed to develop details for her PATH toward her desired result (THERE).

Man's Design – Path of Least Resistance

A man's THP graphic would be more specific by including Genesis 2:5 and 15, Ephesians 5:25-31, and Titus 2:1-8. The HERE rectangle would be changed to represent his current circumstances. The Seven PATH items would remain the same, but details could be added to describe what he would do to fulfill each.

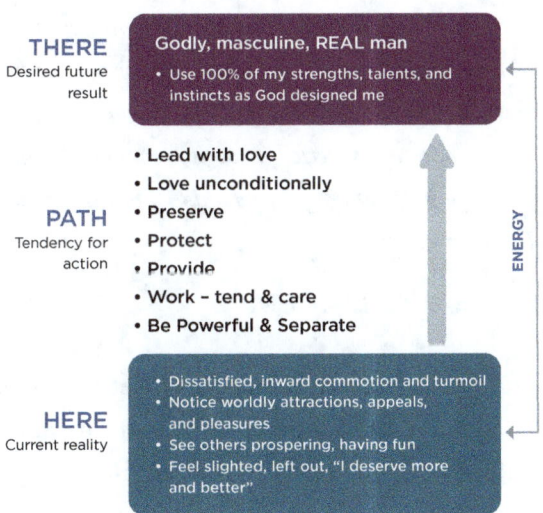

THERE
Desired future result

Godly, masculine, REAL man
• Use 100% of my strengths, talents, and instincts as God designed me

PATH
Tendency for action

• Lead with love
• Love unconditionally
• Preserve
• Protect
• Provide
• Work – tend & care
• Be Powerful & Separate

ENERGY

HERE
Current reality

• Dissatisfied, inward commotion and turmoil
• Notice worldly attractions, appeals, and pleasures
• See others prospering, having fun
• Feel slighted, left out, "I deserve more and better"

When Men and Women focus on their God-given design to become what God wants them to be, He can energize them to move toward their, and His, desired result (THERE).

The issue men and women run into is their carnal, or sin, nature. The apostle Paul describes this.

> *For we know that the law is spiritual, but I am carnal, sold under sin. For what I am doing, I do not understand. For what I will to do, that I do not practice; but what I hate, that I do. If, then, I do what I will not to do, I agree with the law that it is good. But now, it is no longer I who do it, but sin that dwells in me. For I know that in me (that is, in my flesh) nothing good dwells; for to will is present with me, but how to perform what is good I do not find. For the good that I will to do, I do not do; but the evil I will not to do, that I practice. Now if I do what I will not to do, it is no longer I who do it, but sin that dwells in me.*

Romans 7:14-20, NKJV

Paul knows that if he continues to let his sin nature rule, he allows himself to be a slave to sin. It is his, and your, choice as you can see in the following.

*O wretched man that I am! Who will deliver me
from this body of death? I thank God – through
Jesus Christ our Lord!
So then, with the mind I myself serve the law of
God, but with the flesh the law of sin.
There is therefore now no condemnation to
those who are in Christ Jesus, who do not walk
according to the flesh, but according to the Spirit.*

Romans 7:24 – 8:1

That means you will be a real man or woman when
you focus on the way God designed you (THERE) and
allow the Holy Spirit to energize the Godly actions in
the above charts. But if you focus on Flashing your *ME*,
you allow your sin nature to energize your life. That life
creates a competing structure of living in your judgment,
as you will see in book five (*What Damages Relationships*).

Natural Laws that Impact Behavior

An added obstacle to change and living in your
design are the natural laws of entropy and inertia.
They not only impact matter, but they also appear to
affect your behavior. If you look at the THP charts and
consider what Paul says in the above scripture, it is like
these natural laws take over.

That never means you have no control over your
behavior, nor does it give you an excuse to be a victim

of the natural laws. What it does mean is pray for a sensitive conscience to hear the Lord when He wants you to change your thinking. God created the natural laws and as you walk with Him, He prevents or lessens their mental and spiritual impact.

Two Natural Laws—Entropy and Inertia

Entropy is defined as "a measure of the disorder or randomness in a closed system." Entropy is like the inevitable and steady deterioration of a system or society. It sounds complicated, but it is not. Think about a floor that has been swept clean. Will it stay clean? What happens when you drop a stack of cards on the floor? Do they hold together or scatter apart? Do batteries stay charged? Do relationships, even when working well, simply stay that way?

No. Nothing is static. Science tells us that the law of entropy causes things to keep decaying. My speculation is that the concept of entropy comes from the consequences of sin. When you think about entropy, it reminds you about the natural impact of sin, which is ultimately, decay and destruction. And when sin runs its course, it leads to death.

The second natural law of inertia is defined. "A body at rest will tend to stay at rest and a body in motion will tend to stay in motion unless acted on by an external force."

You face the reality of entropy daily, but it is less obvious to you. Inertia is extremely obvious. For example, when you are sitting on the couch watching television, which action is easier: staying put or getting up? It requires more energy to stop what you are doing and get off the couch. Inertia helps you stay put. It takes substantially more energy to *stop* what you are currently doing and move in a *new* direction. The same is true for your life and relationships. It takes more energy to *start* moving in the *right* direction if you are not doing anything. It takes even more energy to *stop* moving in the *wrong* direction and then start moving in the *right* direction!

And here is some great (GR8) news about inertia! Once you start moving in the right direction, it takes less energy to keep moving in that direction. And of course, once you start moving in the *wrong* direction, it takes less energy to continue in that negative direction and acting badly, out of God's plan and design for you.

If you are not putting energy, work, and repetition into all your values, relationships, learning, and improvements, every one of those things will decline because of entropy and inertia.

Look at the graph. It demonstrates the impact of entropy in particular as well as inertia. Business projects have expended billions of hours, dollars and resources making improvements. At the time, the people doing the projects probably felt good about the changes made.

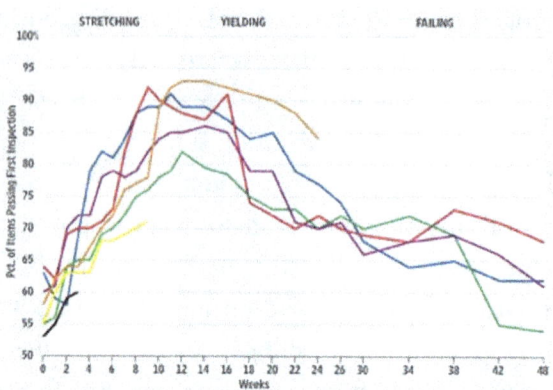

Back Where They Started
Process-Improvement programs often follow the same pattern that a metal spring does when it is pulled with increasing force: They progress through "stretching" and "yielding" phases before failing entirely. Here's a look at the life cycle of seven projects at an aerospace company, with the percentages of items passing first inspection rising initially before turning back down and then returning roughly to original levels.

Where Process-Improvement Projects Go Wrong, Satya S. Chakravorty

In the end, however, each project returned to where they were at the beginning. All because of entropy and inertia.

Your life and relationships will mirror the chart unless you decide to regularly put energy into what you want to accomplish. But do not forget the energy you need the most is from the Lord by way of His Spirit as you walk with Him daily. Do not be the hearer and not the doer, which James speaks about.

But be doers of the word, and not hearers only, deceiving yourselves.

James 1:22, NKJV

The word does not blossom in your life until you apply or do it, especially because your sin nature is working against you. Ezekiel also addresses the topic of doing rather than just hearing. He paints an even better picture of the most common approach to life that Christians take:

> *So they come to you as people do, they sit before you as My people, and they hear your words, but they do not do them; for with their mouth they show much love, but their hearts pursue their own gain.*
>
> **Ezekiel 33:3, NKJV**

That is a clear strategy to enjoy the impact and pain of entropy in your life!

Entropy and Inertia Scenario

As you read the below scenario, think about how entropy and inertia are playing out. At the end of the scenario answer the questions to determine how these two natural laws may be playing out in your life.

Lou, Hal and Andy all work at a small electronics manufacturing firm. Lou and Hal are engineers who report to Andy.

Lou served in the military as an engineer before leaving the service and joining the private sector. He has a high-energy personality and an innovative mind. Hal is pretty laid back and extremely methodical in the way he thinks and acts. Hal and change do not have a very good relationship; he bristles at Lou's constant need to innovate. Andy has a pretty *laissez-faire* attitude toward life and work. He is a hands-off manager, who stays in his office most of the time, attending meetings or talking on the phone. He rarely meets with Lou or Hal, communicating mostly by email.

Lou and Hal are presented with a new project where they have to create a custom design for a large client. The client wants high-tech programming for its smart home and office appliances and fixtures. The client is focused on introducing this new line of products to large residential and commercial builders. These fixtures sometimes need to be retrofitted into existing tech structures in old commercial buildings and older homes, so Lou and Hal need to draw on their years of engineering experience while at the same time inventing innovative products that will work using remote control devices.

Andy always meets with clients, then hands down what they are requesting to Lou and Hal.

In their initial meeting to discuss the project, Lou raises the issue of not working with the client directly, "Andy, you know that we will have a much better result if Hal and I have direct access to the client."

Hal adds, "I'm fine with letting Lou talk to the client and just inform me about what I need to do."

Andy says, "Well, I don't know why we need to change our process. It seems to have worked in the past when I am the one who is client-facing and you guys go do your wizardry." Andy gives Lou a wry smile as he mentions *wizardry*.

Lou reminds Andy of the last big project they worked on, where they were not able to deliver what the client wanted on budget or on the proposed timeline. "We missed both the budget and the deadline with Alpha Computing Services because we were not provided with the correct specs. We need to get in there and talk to the client."

Andy leaned back in his chair and said, "I think this will work fine. I'm not in the mood to change our operating system due to one failed project."

Hal nodded in agreement.

"But we have so many other examples of this. When we don't interact with the client directly, everything in the project starts moving randomly. It's like we don't even know what we are aiming for. If I were going out with my bow and arrow for target practice and I aim at the target and you move it as the arrow is flying through the air, it's near impossible to hit the mark," Lou's irritation with Andy's seemingly *who cares* attitude came through in his tone of voice.

Andy finally said, "Lou, I just think you are over-reacting. I'll have the clients chief engineer email you the specs this afternoon. We have a short development window, so you boys need to get working on it and fast."

Lou cast a glance at Hal, who was looking at something on his phone. Lou thought to himself, "Per usual, Hal is not even engaged or even paying attention."

Andy ends the meeting and says, "Let me know how I can help."

Lou thinks to himself sarcastically, "Like that's going to happen."

Lou and Hal return to their cubicles. Lou immediately starts some research on the little he knows about the project and the challenges of creating what will give the client the results they need. Hal gets on LinkedIn and makes some new connections, then finishes his expense report for the end-of-the-month, then spends the rest of the day answering non-essential emails.

Scenario Questions

1. How do you see Entropy at work in this scenario?

_____

_____

_____

_____

_____

_____

_____

2. How has Entropy impacted this company's
    interactions with clients?

_____

_____

_____

_____

_____

3. How is inertia at work in this scenario?

_____

_____

_____

_____

_____

4. How has it impacted the relationships among
    these three men?

_____

_____

_____

_____

_____

5. What negative consequences can you see
    from the impacts of entropy and inertia in the
    scenario?

_____

_____

_____

_____

_____

6. What actions might you suggest for Lou, Hal
    and Andy?

_____

_____

_____

_____

_____

7. Do you have a working or personal scenario,
    where you see the laws of entropy or inertia
    at work? What are the consequences of the
    current situation? What can you do to move in
    a new and better direction?

_____

_____

_____

_____

God's Image – Foundation for Our Design

Thinking about choosing the right path in life requires that we go back to the basis of design for humankind and specifically men and women. First of all, we were designed in God's image. God planned for man to rule and reign in the earth, but Adam and Eve made some choices that led to the fall of man into a sinful nature. Subsequently, all of us must depend on our PERFECT Father God to show us the right path and make the right choices to live a Godly life.

Let's look at what scripture says about man being made in God's image, and the specific designs God created for man and woman.

> Then God said, "Let Us make man in Our image, according to Our likeness; let them have dominion over the fish of the sea, over the birds of the air, and over the cattle, over all the earth and over every creeping thing that creeps on the earth." So God created man in His own image; in the image of God He created him; male and female He created them. Then God blessed them, and God said to them, "Be fruitful and multiply; fill the earth and subdue it; have dominion over the fish of the sea, over the birds of the air, and over every living thing that moves on the earth."

> **Genesis 1:26-28, NKJV**

This first and foundational passage in scripture articulates God's purpose for creating man. The first part notes that man is made in the image and likeness of God (1:26a). That is reiterated with the added clarity of the distinction of male and female (27). Notice that God was not vague by using terms like gender, which is a made-up word to create the illusion of more options. He clearly stated that mankind was comprised of two categories, "male and female."

If your "Who said so" is God, please do not back away from how He says that he created us. It may require some courage to state the obvious based on the chromosomes of each human being, but God only created "male and female" human beings.

We are created in the "image of God," but please do not distort that to include that we are like God. Nothing and no being are like God. He is separate and holy, which means He is completely different than anything our minds can imagine. Just as images or statues represented deities and kings in the ancient Near East, so man, as the image of God, was created to represent God Himself as the sovereign over all creation.

This bold metaphor is spelled out in Genesis 1:26b, which explains what it means for man to be created in the image of God.

> *Then God said, "Let us make mankind in our image, in our likeness, so that they may rule over*

the fish in the sea and the birds in the sky, over
the livestock and all the wild animals, and over
all the creatures that move along the ground."

Genesis 1:26, NIV

In verse 28, God blesses Adam and Eve, then gives them a mandate.

God blessed them and said to them, "Be fruitful
and increase in number; fill the earth and subdue
it. Rule over the fish in the sea and the birds in
the sky and over every living creature that moves
on the ground."

Genesis 1:28, NIV

Dr. Roy Zuck explains, "The key words in this statement of purpose are the verbs *rule* (1:26, 28) and *subdue* (v. 28). So, man is created to reign in a way that demonstrates His lordship, His domination, by force if necessary, over all creation."[1]

Now if that is true, the creation of man and woman is part of the theological center of the Bible. That means we must clearly understand the creation of man and woman, so we have clarity about how and for what purpose they were created. But first, consider what Dr. Zuck says.

He states that man is created in the image of God to do the following.

- Represent God Himself as the sovereign over all creation
- Reign in a manner that demonstrates his lordship, his domination, by force, if necessary, over all creation

Consider that man is not only to show his lordship, his domination, but also to rule as a representative of God Himself, implies stewardship.

God put man here to rule, reign and have dominion, but that changed when Eve and Adam chose to follow Satan's plan not God's. Satan's deception of Eve and the ultimate disobedience by both Adam and Eve put the rule of the earth under Satan. He is now the ruler of this world. He is the one with dominion as you can see in these verses.

> *Now is the judgment of this world; now the ruler of this world will be cast out.*

John 12:31, NKJV

> *. . . of judgment, because the ruler of this world is judged.*

John 16:11, NKJV

Since man's sin somehow put Satan in as ruler, God's plan of salvation will ultimately reestablish mankind as the ruler. So, consider salvation this way; it is deliverance from one place or state to another. That means salvation takes mankind from the current status back to the original plan.

Therefore, while salvation is an awesome gift by our gracious Father, it is not the central theme of God's Word. Man's creation to be ruler of this world is the central theme and salvation is the amazing instrument God uses to revoke Satan's rule and hand it back to mankind.

This underscores the importance of Genesis. Unfortunately, it is too easy to see the first few chapters in Genesis as only the story of beginnings, but it is vastly more important, especially for relationships and marriage. In fact, the first three chapters of Genesis tell us the following, and more:

- Man's creation and design (what he was designed to do).
- Woman's creation and design (what she was designed to do).
- Foundation used for both of those designs.
- Importance of and how designs are used in marriage.
- Contract for Godly marriage.
- Blueprint for how we sin.
- Structure we follow as the path of least resistance to sin.

- Problems for marriages when not following God's roles.
- God's Judgment on Women (Curse) and its impact on relationships and life.
- God's Judgment on Men (Curse) and its impact on relationships and life.

Genesis is critical to understanding the entirety of God's revelation. It provides the *how* and *why*.

REFLECTIVE QUESTIONS

- How does God's image play into the creation of man and woman?

_____

_____

_____

_____

- Looking at what happened when Adam and Eve believed the serpent and disobeyed God, who were they focusing on?

_____

_____

_____

_____

- Thinking about your life and your relationship with God, are you headed down the right path?

_____

_____

_____

_____

Men and Women's Designs

Genesis provides the *how* and *why* foundation for understanding the design for men and women. God's whole purpose throughout the Bible is to bring mankind back into the purpose of God's original design, which is to rule and reign over the earth with Him.

Let's look more closely at God's specific design of men and women and the purpose that each of them serves. Then, we will look at the unknown judgments for men and women. All of this impacts the challenges that all of us have in choosing the right path to glorifying God and godliness.

Man's Design and Purpose

Looking at Genesis chapter 2, God provides insight into the design of men and women. The following verses indicate the specific reasons God created man.

> . . . *before any plant of the field was in the earth and before any herb of the field had grown. For the Lord God had not caused it to rain on the earth, and there was no man to till the ground; but a mist went up from the earth and watered the whole face of the ground. And the Lord God formed man of the dust of the ground and breathed into his nostrils the breath of life; and man became a living being. Then*

the Lord God took [a]the man and put him in
the garden of Eden to tend and keep it.

Genesis 2:5-7, 15, NJKV

In these verses we see that there was no man to *till* the ground or *work* the ground. God put man in the Garden to *tend* and *keep* it. In the Hebrew tend means to labor, work, serve and till. The word *keep* is translated *to have charge of, protect or preserve.* So, it is clear that man is designed for work and activity. That doesn't mean every man is literally working in farming or gardening, so there is a broader implication. The first verb in verse 15, is translated as *tend, work, dress, or cultivate.* In Hebrew, this definition implies, *labor, work, serve, till* and sometimes means *enslavement.*

Here's what Webster's Dictionary says,

- Tend: to be in charge of, manage, operate, to take care of.
- Work: physical or mental effort directed toward doing or making something.
- Dress: to till and cultivate land, apply fertilizer, prune, and trim.
- Cultivate: till, prepare land for growth; plant, tend, harvest, or improve (plants) by labor and skill.

The second verb in the verse, *keep,* is translated keep or take care of. In Hebrew the definition is *have*

charge of, protect, preserve, watch, guard or restrain.
Webster's Dictionary definitions are:

- Keep – to protect, guard, or defend; to
  have, take charge or care of, to look after,
  maintain for use.
- Take care – careful or serious attention,
  protective or supervisory control, to
  provide physical needs, help, or comfort.

Guarding and protecting obviously require labor, effort, or work, but they also have a relational element to them, which implies that man can relate. A more speculative implication is Adam was created first with both powerful and relational capabilities and when Eve was created, most of the relational elements were taken from Adam and placed into Eve. That is speculation, but it does lead us to the creation of Eve.

God looks at the man He created and tells us something profound. He says that man's aloneness was not good. That statement shows that God is relational to make the statement about Adam, and wants what is best for Adam, a suitable companion. God saw Adam's need and met it with His perfect provision.

> *And the Lord God said, "It is not good that*
> *man should be alone; I will make him a helper*
> *comparable to him." Out of the ground the Lord*
> *God formed every beast of the field and every*

*bird of the air, and brought them to Adam to see
what he would call them. And whatever Adam
called each living creature, that was its name. So
Adam gave names to all cattle, to the birds of the
air, and to every beast of the field. But for Adam
there was not found a helper comparable to him.*

Genesis 2:18-20, NKJV

Notice that God did not speak about Adam's
feelings or opinion in this situation. God saw Adam's
need, just like God sees our needs and knows them
before we do. Adam was probably like many men today
who are blissfully ignorant of the fact that they need
a helper. Unfortunately, when men treat their wives
improperly and don't value their role, they are in a sense
saying to God, "I despise your gift."

Finally, God's design of man included oneness
with woman.

*Therefore a man shall leave his father and mother
and be joined to his wife, and they shall become
one flesh.*

Genesis 2:24, NKJV

Man's need for companionship clearly shows that
the combination of man and woman's design is good.
Looking at the foundation of man and woman's design,

it's clear their designs complement each other. Man's design works best when a woman is included and vice versa.

That speaks directly against the world's view of same sex relationships. Being the same is not complementary. God did not create two men or two women, He created man and woman so they could be "fruitful and multiply" and have dominion over the earth.

Woman's Design and Purpose

And the Lord God said, "It is not good that man should be alone; I will make him a helper comparable to him."

Genesis, 2:18, NKJV

God designed woman because man needed a helper who was comparable to him. He actually created her out of Adam's flesh. Many people think that the role and value of *helper* is less than the one who needs the help. That is what Satan wants people to believe. If women do not have the same role as men, they must not have the same value. That is the same lie he tells everyone, everywhere: If you do not have a large or prestigious role, it means you are less valuable as a person.

If you understand the *way* God uses the word helper it can be humbling and amazing for both men and women. The Hebrew word used is *ezer,* and it occurs in the Bible 21 times. It means help, support, aid and designates assistance, or more often assistant. God actually describes Himself as a helper through the psalmist. Look at Psalm 121.

will lift up my eyes to the hills—
From whence comes my help?
My help comes from the Lord,
Who made heaven and earth.

Psalm 121:1-2, NKJV

So being designated as a helper puts you in good company! Being a helper is a high calling and what women are made for. In essence the helper looks at life through God's eyes and acts like God because her role elevates service over self. Again, she is not less-than, just in a different role.

Woman is also made in God's Image. She is designed for relationships and helping, which is not demeaning or derogatory. Her design indicates her need for belonging and relationships. She tends to need safety and security as well.

God is the perfect creator. He knows precisely how things, and people, fit together best, and He created woman as the perfect companion for man.

To summarize the complementary design and purpose of men and women, let's look at their roles. Men are designed to work to provide, protect and preserve, and women are designed to help, nurture and support. The two roles perfectly complement each other, just as God planned it.

UNKNOWN JUDGMENTS FOR MEN AND WOMEN

As you may have read in the book from this series, *What Damages Relationships?*, men and women are plagued with judgments tied to their designs. God designed men and women for His purposes and so that they could relate to Him and each other, reflecting Him. At the same time, He proclaimed judgment that relates to the way He designed them.

Unknown Judgment for Women

Let's see what He said in His Word regarding His judgment of women.

> *To the woman He said: "I will greatly multiply your sorrow and your conception;*
> *In pain you shall bring forth children;*
> *Your desire shall be for your husband,*
> *And he shall rule over you."*

Genesis 3:16, NKJV

At GR8 Relationships we call this the Unknown Judgment for Women based on the fact that so many people are not aware of this judgment. Unfortunately, people sum it up by saying some relationships are *just complicated*. People sometimes accept that a relationship *is what it is*, when a deeper understanding of the unknown judgment could help improve the relationship. Common misconceptions about relationships can be found in day-to-day conversations and in the movies or television programs. Often you will hear someone say, "Our relationship is complicated," or "Our relationship is complex."

What about you? Do you think relationships are complicated? Particularly do you view your own relationships as complicated? Most of the time complexity is the result of incorrect thinking about relationships. They are not as complex when you live in them correctly. Relationships are complex when people in relationships focus on themselves instead of others.

The fact is relationships become complex when you make everything about *ME* (yourself) instead of pursuing the other person's best and doing what God asks you to do. Complexity and confusion occur when you are tied up in unhealthy thinking, which leads to toxic feelings and inappropriate actions. They are never complex when doing what the Almighty God asks you to do.

Simplifying relationships focuses on you doing what God wants from you. Doing relationships God's way works. Obeying God is always straightforward and simple; you either are obeying Him or not. When you are not willing to trust that He knows more than you do, you will second-guess Him. You might even find yourself saying to God, "You, want me to forgive him!? You can't mean that God, after what he has done to me."

Let's get to the core of the *Unknown Judgments about Women*. This will clear up a lot of misconceptions and *bad thinking*, which leads to poor feelings and actions.

The context of the conversation in Genesis 3:16 is a conversation between the serpent and Eve.:

> *. . . the woman saw that the tree was good for*
> *food, that it was pleasant to the eyes, and*
> *a tree desirable to make one wise, she took the*
> *fruit and ate. She also gave to her husband with*
> *her, and he ate.*

Genesis 3:6, NKJV

Immediately after Adam and Eve sinned by doing the one thing God forbid them to do in the Garden, they realized they were naked, made clothes out of fig leaves and tried to hide from God. When God confronted them, they tried to blame everyone but themselves, which only led to judgments, first to the Serpent, then Eve, then Adam. Here we will only deal with the curses toward Eve and Adam.

To reiterate, here is the curse toward Eve.

> *To the woman He said: "I will greatly multiply*
> *your sorrow and your conception;*
> *In pain you shall bring forth children;*
> *Your desire shall be for your husband,*
> *And he shall rule over you."*

Genesis 3:16, NKJV

This judgment is tough! God designed a woman to be relational, but this judgment now makes it difficult to fulfill her relational design.

Ladies, if you experience these problems daily, you are not doing what God asks you to do. By His grace you have a solution, but if you are not paying attention your sin nature will drive you to live in your judgment.

Three Elements of Woman's Judgment

The three judgments women must deal with are, Pain with Children, Desire for Her Husband, and Ruled by Her Husband. Let's look at each of these more closely.

Pain with Children

Pain with children comes with their birth and raising them.

The word *pain* means painful toil. Any woman who has been through labor having a baby can attest to the toil required. Consider Jabez's mother and her childbirth. She says,

> *Now Jabez was more honorable than his brothers,*
> *and his mother called his name Jabez, saying,*
> *Because I bore him in pain.*

1 Chronicles 4:9, NKJV

Childbirth was so painful for her that she named her child after it!

As Matthew Henry, author of an exhaustive commentary on the Bible, so aptly describes, a mother's pains of raising children can last for years. He says,

> *"The sorrows of child-bearing are multiplied;*
> *for they include, not only the travailing throes,*
> *but the indispositions before (it is sorrow from*
> *the conception), and the nursing toils and*
> *vexations after; and after all, if the children prove*
> *wicked and foolish, they are, more than ever,*
> *the heaviness of her that bore them. Thus are the*

*sorrows multiplied; as one grief is over, another
succeeds in this world."*

Matthew Henry[2]

Though the news of this judgment against women
is heavy, the good news is that God has a solution.
Following His plan for living life and focusing on what
you need to do to counteract the natural tendency
toward succumbing to the judgment. It goes back to
focusing on the highest and best for others.

Desire for Her Husband

Here are the two interpretations of this point that
are most prevalent.

1. She so craves a relationship with her husband
   that she will do anything to have it. Some
   commentaries interpret this as "a strong
   sexual and psychological dependence on her
   husband."
2. She wants to make the relationship go her way.
   She wants the husband to do whatever she
   wants him to do.

The first interpretation can be supported by
the strong desire that a woman can have to enjoy a
relationship with a man. She is wired to be relational,
and it makes sense that she could be consumed with

that desire, which could make life miserable when her husband is not responding. In addition, the interpretation is supported when the word for *desire* in Hebrew (*tsuka*) is taken from the Aramaic root for *exciting, loving, or psychological desire.*

Most of the time, men have the stronger desire for sexual fulfillment than women, which does not mean a woman would not want or enjoy sex, but a woman *craving* sex in the relationship is an anomaly. This fact can present difficulty with the first interpretation.

The second interpretation can be more easily supported when the word for *desire* in Hebrew (*tsuka*) is stated as coming from the Aramaic root that means *to compel, to urge, to seek control.*

Additionally, when you look for other occurrences of *tsuka* it shows up in the next chapter of Genesis when God was talking with Cain about his anger for the Lord not respecting his offering.

> *If you do well, will you not be accepted? And if you do not do well, sin lies at the door. And its desire is for you, but you should rule over it.*

Genesis 4:7, NKJV

Here *desire* is similar to a predator stalking its prey, ready to pounce, the same picture the Lord gives us about Satan.

Whether you agree with the first or second interpretation, you will end up in the same place.

When you crave a relationship, or have an unhealthy dependence on it, you will use a stealth strategy to achieve the relationship you need. So, you manipulate others to get your way. You will be wearing a mask, controlling others without being obvious. It will appear that you are doing what they want, but you are trying to get what you want. It doesn't appear controlling although it is.

On the other hand, when you dominate the relationship through aggression, you use force or power as your strategy to create the relationship that meets your needs. You have learned techniques that work for this strategy, especially when the other person does not put up a fight.

Either strategy leads to *control*. Ultimately, the woman living in her judgment does not want to follow or live under the authority of her husband. This is the consequence of not listening to the Lord and not following what He has shown you to do in His Word.

Though you may not agree with this conclusion, plenty of anecdotal evidence supports it, likely in your own experience. Objectively look at your own behavior over time to see what is true about this conclusion in the way that you act.

Ruled by Her Husband

The last element of a woman's judgment provides additional news on how your husband with relate to you. Look at the part of verse 16.

. . . and he shall rule over you.

Genesis 3:16c, NKJV

Rule is the critical word in this phrase. The Hebrew word is *mashal*, which means to have dominion, reign govern, master, gain control, or have authority. Here are two common interpretations.

1. The verse is a restatement of man's authority that the Lord has already provided. This is God's order for the family and it is reaffirmed in 1 Corinthians 11:3 that talks about God, Christ, man and woman.

   But I want you to know that the head of every man is Christ, the head of woman is man, and the head of Christ is God.

   1 Corinthians 11:3, NKJV

2. It can indicate harshness, abuse or using the relationship for personal benefit. In Genesis 2, you see that Adam was designated as the authority, to rule.

This is also evident in his judgment from God, "because you have listened to your wife . . ."

And it is evident in the way Adam named Eve as well as the animals. When you name something, you have authority over them.

While authority already belonged to Adam, using that authority and acting harshly toward women would be new now that Adam and Eve had sinned. Before the sin, there was no evidence that Adam was harsh. But, the history of the world reveals a testimony of man's abuse of authority and women.

Both interpretations combined provide reality. Man is the authority at home, as we see in 1 Corinthians 11:3, and he is the ruler, even if and when his wife is controlling him. He has this assigned role from God, not because he deserves it, because God sees it as the best for order. Since man is selfish, his rule won't always be as healthy or appropriate as God intended.

Unknown Judgment for Men

When you view what God tells you through the window of relationships, it makes His Word even more practical and understandable. The judgments are particularly helpful to me because the effects are so easy to see. But the judgments are not taught in a way to help people see them in relationships and marriages. Unfortunately, they are too often unknown or ignored.

Genesis 3:16-19 will impact every man and woman on the face of the earth until Christ comes again. Each and every relationship struggle has a link back to these judgments. It has proven true in most (probably *all*) of the discussions that Louie and I have had with couples that are struggling in their relationship.

Unfortunately, like so much of God's Word, people do not consider it relevant for today or just no longer in effect. You may refer to Genesis as that "creation story part of the Bible," but the designs and judgments are real. These judgments impact your life right now unless you are walking with the Lord and doing what He asks *real* men and women to do.

Next, the man's judgment is described below:

> *Then to Adam He said, "Because you have heeded the voice of your wife, and have eaten from the tree of which I commanded you, saying, 'You shall not eat of it': Cursed is the ground for your sake in toil you shall eat of it all the days of your life. Both thorns and thistles it shall bring forth for you, and you shall eat the herb of the field. In the sweat of your face you shall eat bread till you return to the ground, for out of it you were taken; for dust you are, and to dust you shall return."*

Genesis 3:17, NKJV

Essentially, what you see in this passage is what Adam did to create his problems and the how his judgments would impact him. First, he listened to someone besides God when deciding what action to take, and therefore sinned. Second, the ground is cursed, which now requires pain and sweat for Adam in order to eat and provide for his family. Third, all his hard work and toil that drives him will only lead back to dust.

Adam's Curse

There are three elements that God states in the judgment issued to Adam. He followed and did not lead when Eve gave the forbidden fruit to him. The second one was not a direct curse to Adam. The ground was cursed, which causes the third element, Adam's toil will be painful and he would be returned to dust.

Again, remember the context. Adam and Eve sinned, God issued a judgment on Satan and Eve, now He turns to Adam. God does all things perfectly, right? So, the very order in which He pronounces the judgments is important.

Followed, Didn't Lead

When God issued the judgment to Adam (starting in verse 17) it seems to me He is saying this:

> *"Finally, Adam, you were given the authority to have dominion with Eve over the entire earth. Instead, you abdicated your leadership, listened*

to, and followed Eve, not Me, and now this
entire earth is cursed to be under the dominion of
Satan."

Scripture specifically states that Eve was deceived, but Adam was not (1 Timothy 2:14). Unfortunately, many scholars assume that is a good comment about Adam and, therefore, blame Eve for sin. That misses the gravity of Adam's sin.

If you looked at this conversation as a human father talking to his son, it might be, "Adam, you and I had a clear conversation about My expectations for you and Eve. You knew you were not to eat of the Tree of the Knowledge of Good and Evil, but you did it anyway. There are terrible consequences for disobedience and it's going to be painful!"

Like the woman's judgment, the more you understand this judgment, the more aware you will be on how much it affects your life and then, hopefully, turn to and choose God's way instead. Since you have read about the woman's judgment, you already have some insight about what God will be doing with the man's judgment.

The first, and probably the most important, lesson for men is the reason God issued the judgment. If you have not let the first part of verse 17 grab your attention, please read it slowly.

. . . you have heeded the voice of your wife, and
have eaten of the tree of which I commanded you,
saying, "you shall not eat of it.".

Genesis 3:17a, NKJV

Here is an especially important question for you, which ties directly to God's statement to Adam. Who is your "*Who said so?*" Adam knew the *Who said so,* and chose to replace God with Eve. Are you doing something similar in your life? Is your *Who said so* someone or something other than God?

Your answer to that question lies in what you value and where you spend your time and money. You know the correct answer is God, and probably even say it, but the reality of your time and money shows you the truth. Unfortunately, getting along with others, especially with your wife, can easily become more important than dealing with difficult issues, listening to God, and doing what He says is the right thing to do.

The common sayings, "Happy wife, happy life!" or "If momma isn't happy, nobody is happy!" may be the way a lot of relationships work, but that does not make them right. In fact, those sayings likely mean you are not leading, just like Adam did not lead.

The first part of the man's judgment can easily be distorted and has been by those with an agenda against women. It is not hard to imagine someone teaching that a husband does not need to listen to his wife because he is the head of the home and makes all decisions. Of course, that is foolishness, easily debunked by the verse itself and by the way that God has called a man to love his wife.

> *Husbands, love your wives, just as Christ also loved the church and gave Himself for her, that He might sanctify and cleanse her with the washing of water by the word, that He might present her to Himself a glorious church, not having spot or wrinkle or any such thing, but that she should be holy and without blemish. So husbands ought to love their own wives as their own bodies; he who loves his wife loves himself. For no one ever hated his own flesh, but nourishes and cherishes it, just as the Lord does the church. 30 For we are members of His body of His flesh and of His bones. For this reason a man shall leave his father and mother and be joined to his wife, and the two shall become one flesh.*

Ephesians 5:25-31, NKJV

The words most commonly used in the various translations to describe the conversation between Adam and Eve are *listened to*, except for a couple that use *heeded*. In the older translations the words used are *hearkened unto*.

The full impact of the problem is not adequately stated when you only read the words *listened to*, because most people think of it as *hearing* someone. The word listen is defined in a variety of ways, as listed below.

- to hear (perceive by ear); to hear of or concerning; to hear (have power to hear); to hear. with attention or interest, listen to; to hear (of judicial cases).
- to understand (language).
- to grant request.
- to listen, give heed, to listen to.
- to consent, agree, yield to, to obey, be obedient.

When you consider the gravity of the situation, the last item on the above list: "to consent, agree, yield to, to obey, be obedient" is appropriate. Use of any lesser terms does not convey the gravity of what God was telling Adam.

God is clearly telling Adam, "I am declaring a judgment on you because you followed Eve, not Me, and that further means you were not leading."

The picture I get in my mind is a private saluting an officer.

Adam was saluting Eve and saying, "Yes, ma'am! I'll eat it ma'am!"

Obviously, that picture is a bit over-the-top, but it is much more in line with the context than Adam just listening to what Eve said. The context is about hearing then doing or acting on what Eve told him to do instead of doing what God told him to do.

Adam's judgment was clearly a result of him obeying the wrong person or the wrong *Who said so*. It has less to do with Adam hearing something and more to do with his will and the decision he made based on what he heard and who said it to him.

Remember the additional context of this passage. This sin in the Garden of Eden happened in the context of a marriage gone wrong. Adam was not protecting Eve and leading her, he was following her, obeying her, and leaving her open and vulnerable. The fact is, you cannot obey and lead the same person at the same time!

The judgment then adds more condemnation on Adam: he was *not* deceived, yet he willingly followed his wife into sin. Let's see what the Apostle Paul says about that.

> *And Adam was not deceived, but the woman being deceived, fell into transgression.*

1 Timothy 2:14, NKJV

He was much more the sinner in this situation than Eve because he was not deceived; at least Eve had that as an excuse. Adam had heard the command directly from God because Eve had not been created when that command was given by God. He knew the command and had no valid excuse because he was not even deceived by the serpent. He acted based on what Eve said, the one he was supposed to protect and provide for.

The Ground is Cursed

The second element is that the ground is cursed. If you stop there, that may not sound that bad for Adam, but God follows with four new things that will now be part of Adam's, and your, existence.

One: Toil will be required in order to eat.
Two: Thorns and thistles will grow from the ground.
Three: Herbs of the field will be a food source.
Four: Sweat will be required to eat bread.

Though the curse was not directly placed on Adam, it would cause him pain throughout his life. God created this amazing, perfect environment of the Garden of Eden and the entire earth. Now, the very thing that God told Adam and Eve to take dominion over, recounted in Genesis 1:28, rebels against them.

You may have noticed a difference in the woman's and man's judgment. The woman was judged directly. Her very nature and being was judged. With the man, his nature and being were indirectly judged through the curse that God placed on the ground.

What does it mean that the ground is cursed? The ground will no longer participate with Adam in accomplishing the work to be done. Before the judgment, Adam did not need fertilizer. The seed that was planted would grow, and no matter what Adam did the growth of the seed would continue to go in the right direction. No weeds grew. The ground partnered perfectly with him. But after the curse, the ground became hostile to his efforts and work!

So, Adam would now have pain in his work. The earth that Adam had to work or tend and keep became hostile and would no longer easily respond. The lack of response from the ground created *toil* for Adam. That word *toil* in Hebrew only occurs three times in the Bible, and it occurs first in Genesis 3:16. It is the same word used for the pain that a woman will have in childbirth.

A woman experiences pain in her relationships. A man feels pain in his work. Our perfect God created the perfect judgments. Both man and woman have pain, and that pain is directly linked to the judgments God placed on them respectively.

Men deal with this pain differently. Some men give up because of the pain and become irresponsible. Others work harder trying to beat the pain and become workaholics. But none ever control their work. The weeds always grow back; what was done, becomes undone again.

From Dust to Dust

Finally, the ground will take him back as dust. The earth or dust was what Adam was created from and he will now die and turn back to dust.

Men, this judgment attacks you at your core. God designed you with a need to be significant, but the judgment works directly against that need. Its effect reinforces the reality that you were made from dust and you will return to it. All the work you do will eventually need to be redone.

The law of entropy prevails. As we discussed earlier, entropy is a measure of the disorder or randomness in a closed system. Inevitable and steady deterioration of a system or society. Both judgments reinforce entropy, a disorder in relationships for women and in work for men, which is the way sin works in and on all of us and God's creation.

Just like the woman's judgment, God did not leave you without a way out. He has a solution. Every invitation and instruction that He has given to men about how He wants you to think, act, and feel is part of His solution to your judgment. Obviously, the solution starts with the inner working of the life of Christ, but it requires a choice to live for righteousness not unrighteousness.

The Judgment is *reality*. You and I may not like it but this is the way that it is, not just how it feels. Not wanting it to be this way is a typical method of trying to remove the pain, but it does not work. It is reality, and it does not feel good. Whether you agree or not, it does not make it untrue. People can tell you about your lack of leadership in the home, unhealthy focus on establishing your identity based on your work and activities, but you are the one to do something about it. Are you willing to see this as real or just deny it?

Your judgment as a man will focus your attention on work and activities, but the ground will not cooperate, and it will take pain and sweat to produce results. Without doing life God's way, work will be painful and unfulfilling.

That difficulty at work will combine with the judgment on women to create further relationship problems. The more difficult the relationships, the more you may focus on work to be "significant" there, because you are not feeling or just are not significant at home.

You can unlock the solution by accepting the way that God has designed men and God's description of a real man in Titus 2, which includes the solution for all relationships.

Work and Providing

Please note that work is not the curse, it just leads back to dust; work is no longer fulfilling as it was before the fall. To get the full impact of this judgment, do you remember how Adam—and all men—are designed? Go back to chapter 2 in Genesis:

> *Before any plant of the field was in the earth and before any herb of the field had grown. For the*

Lord God had not caused it to rain on the earth, and there was no man to till the ground

Genesis 2:5, NKJV

Then the Lord God took the man and put him in the garden of Eden to tend and keep it.

Genesis 2:15, NKJV

Why is looking at our design so important? Man's judgment directly impacts his design! Just like the woman's relational design is impacted by her judgment, the same linkage is true for man and his design and judgment.

Note: This information will show up again in book seven in this series because this information is crucial to understanding how to pursue their best!

REFLECTIVE QUESTIONS

For Men

- Think of the first part of Adam's judgment, that he followed what Eve said instead of following God's instruction. Have you made choices like that? What was the consequence?

_____

_____

_____

_____

- Think of the second part of the judgment, that the ground is cursed. How is that impacting your life right now? What choices do you have to make to deal with that?

_____

_____

_____

_____

- Based on the third part of the judgment (that man came from dust and will be returned to

dust), how does that impact your attitude
toward your work? How does that impact your
feeling of significance? What does this third
part imply for your relationship with others,
and especially God?

_____

_____

_____

_____

For Women

• Based on man's judgment that he followed what
  Eve said instead of what God commanded),
  what if anything can you change in the way that
  you relate to people in important relationships
  in your life? Are there different paths than the
  one you are on that you need to take?

_____

_____

_____

_____

• How can you support others who you are in a
  relationship with?

_____

_____

_____

_____

- Stand in your husband or betrothed's shoes, how do you notice the concept of dust to dust impacting him? This part (and the painful toil) directly impact a man's desire for significance. How can you help, not nag, him to pursue significance at home instead of primarily through work and activities?

_____

_____

_____

_____

CURRENT REALITY AND DESIRED FUTURE

The path for each of your relationships is basically broken, or restoring. A broken path in a relationship includes selfishness, not serving others, and it ignores the true status of relationships. No one is immune from relationships being broken. On the other hand, a restoring path for relationships moves it toward a desired future. This path includes forgiveness, reconciliation, love, trust, and renewed respect. This path can create a new direction for relationships whether they are between husband and wife, siblings, parents and children or among business colleagues.

Your Relationships – Broken or Restoring

As noted earlier in this book when your focus in life is to satisfy yourself rather than glorify God, your relationships with others in your life will be impacted.

Anytime you make life about *ME* you are going against what God intended for relationships.

> *Do you not know that to who you present*
> *yourselves slaves to obey, you are that one's slaves*
> *whom you obey, whether of sin leading to death,*
> *or of obedience leading to righteousness?*

Romans 6:16, NKJV

When you are not in God's Word, hearing and doing what He says, your autopilot becomes sin and selfishness. You might be uncomfortable admitting that, but it is the truth and reality. Robert Fritz, whose insights have been major contributors to GR8 Relationships, says, "Reality is an acquired taste." He is right.

Relationships are easily broken, but the good news is there is hope for restoring them. No relationship is beyond hope unless you choose that. The restoration path is less traveled, but always the best path for any relationship. Perhaps you are tempted right now to simply abandon your troubled relationship instead of trusting it to God and investing the energy needed to restore it. If you can resist that temptation and open your mind to the concepts and practices we use at GR8 Relationships (to accept others fully for who they are, walking in forgiveness and confession), you will see that reconciliation is totally possible. Then you can experience love, joy, peace, and the remainder of the fruit of the

Spirit in ways that you never thought possible. Whatever relationship you want to restore, it is best with the commitment from both parties. When both parties to a relationship decide to pursue the best for each other patiently, kindly, sacrificially and unconditionally, they operate the way that God relates to them.

> *If you keep My commandments, you will abide in My love, just as I have kept My Father's commandments and abide in His love.*
>
> **John 15:10, NKJV**

On the other hand, if you decide to say *yes* to God in the midst of a broken relationship that is going the wrong way, there is still hope for restoration. In those times, you do what is right despite the behavior of others because that is how Jesus acts with you. So, you say *yes*, even when they say *no*!

Be as honest and objective as possible when you assess which path your relationships are on. Look and see if they are getting better, staying the same or getting worse. That is the first step to moving a relationship down the right path.

Objectivity

Unfortunately, the decision to save or abandon a relationship is often based on how people feel. Feelings create a poor foundation for decisions because they are subjective and untrustworthy.

You can feel good about doing bad and feel bad about doing good, can't you?

Many times, we have counseled couples where neither *felt* like restoring the relationship. So, GR8 Relationships starts with helping people renew their minds with truth so they can see the reality that they can *choose* to move the relationship to the better path of restoration.

Some people will tell you to "follow your heart," which can be harmful if it is taken to mean "follow your feelings." Following your heart isn't always the wrong thing to do, because feelings contribute to making life great when they are linked to great thinking. But if feelings are tied to opinion or lies, watch out. Consider the below verse from Jeremiah.

> *The heart is deceitful above all things and desperately wicked, who can know it?*

Jeremiah 17:9, NKJV

To be objective you see the situation clearly so you can make wise decisions. When you are objective, you do not interpret events, you observe truth and facts. In relationships objectivity is a challenge since each person who is a party to the relationship has their own perspective. This leads to many conversations never progressing past the *he said, she said* level. Failure to see a relationship objectively leads to negative consequences, so how can you better see objectively? By seeing reality with new eyes, the way God sees.

> *Trust in the Lord with all your heart and lean*
> *not on your own understanding. In all your ways*
> *acknowledge Him and He will direct your paths*

Proverbs 3:5-6, NKJV

To develop objective thinking, break reality into separate elements. Consider this Chinese proverb to help you analyze your thinking:

> *The men of old . . . first set up good government*
> *in their own states; wanting good government*
> *in their states, they first established order in*
> *their own families; wanting order in the home,*
> *they first disciplined themselves; desiring self-*
> *discipline, they rectified their own hearts; and*
> *wanting to rectify hearts, they sought precise*
> *verbal definitions of their inarticulate thoughts.*

The topic of good government was too large, so they broke it down, all the way to definitions in the statements. The same is true for you. First you assess your thoughts, which you can do by examining the definitions of the words you use. When you have solid definitions for love and forgiveness you will have good thinking that will produce appropriate actions.

Objective Thinking Scenario

As you read the following scenario, notice where you see objective thinking and where you see thinking driven by opinions, assumptions, and speculation. Then answer the questions at the end of the scenario.

Andrew and Miriam have worked in the same software development company for 15 years. They worked as peers on the same team at one time and developed a caustic relationship. It got so bad that Andrew found a position in a different division of the company. Two months ago, the company reorganized so now Andrew reports to Miriam. He is not happy about that but coming to work every day with the best attitude he can muster, so he can produce excellent work.

It's Tuesday morning, time for the weekly project status update. Andrew arrives early to the conference room and opens his laptop to clear up some emails while he waits for everyone to arrive. Jill arrives next, quickly greets Andrew then glues herself to her phone while waiting for the meeting to start. Roberto arrives next and tries to strike up a conversation with Jill, who doesn't seem interested in the small talk. Amber, who is typically quiet and thoughtful in meetings arrives with her notebook and pen and smiles at everyone without saying anything. Miriam races into the room to the front of the conference room table and places her laptop and notebook firmly on the table. She hurriedly sits down to start the meeting.

Before she can say anything, Andrew thinks to himself, "Good grief, if Miriam wouldn't overbook herself to meetings, maybe she wouldn't be so frantic all the time."

Miriam starts by apologizing, "I apologize for being the last one here. All of you are so prompt, and always arrive early to the meeting," she says with a smile. "Did everyone receive the agenda that Mary Lou sent out yesterday?"

Everyone nods and either pulls it up on their laptop or refers to a printed copy.

"So, let's start with item 1 on the agenda. Roberto has an update from our new client team."

Roberto smiles at everyone, shares his PowerPoint deck on the conference room screen and quickly runs through the slides describing the new client that just started working with his team. "I think you are all going to like working with this client. When I met with their IT department last week I found them easy to talk to. I didn't feel any animosity or push-back from anyone on their team about allowing us to help them solve their payroll process issues."

Andrew asks, "What did they do that indicated there was no animosity or push-back?"

Roberto said, "Good question Andrew, they just all nodded their heads a lot and no one interrupted me at all as I led the meeting."

Andrew said, "That's great that the meeting went smoothly. What questions did you ask to verify that they were tracking with what you were saying?"

Roberto said, "Well, I didn't feel I needed to because the atmosphere was so positive."

Andrew nodded his head and didn't ask any further questions. He could sense that Roberto was getting agitated at his questions, so he figured Roberto must feel insecure about what the client was thinking or if they were really agreeing with him. Andrew thought to himself, "I would have asked more questions. You don't want to get blindsided by a client who is acting like they agree when they could be plotting against you."

"Thanks for the good report, Roberto," Miriam said. "Next we will hear from Andrew."

"Thanks Miriam. I do not have a PowerPoint because most of my reporting from Piper Production is Excel spreadsheet driven. I've prepared a printed document for you," he said as he passed the handouts to each person at the table.

Miriam warns, "Andrew, you are only allotted 5 minutes. It looks like it will take you 30 to get through all this."

Andrew feels his face turn red and wishes his annoyance with Miriam wasn't so obvious. "Miriam, why don't you just trust me and kick me out of the meeting if I talk too long."

An awkward silence blankets the room as other team members are not sure how to react to this obvious dislike between Andrew and Miriam.

"Sorry Andrew, continue."

Andrew talks through the summary page at the back of the handout. Then taps his iPhone and declares that he only spent 4 minutes and 55 seconds.

Miriam smiles wryly and barely shakes her head, amused at Andrews antics. The meeting continues until everyone has reported on their projects and all issues have been discussed.

Later that day Amber and Jill meet for lunch to discuss weekend plans they have for their families to go to the country together.

"Gosh, did you see how rude Andrew was to Roberto and to Miriam? What is his problem anyway?" Jill said as they waited for their order to arrive.

Amber smiled quietly and said, "I don't know, maybe he doesn't like it that he isn't in charge. These exchanges between him and others on the team always makes me uncomfortable."

"It just makes me mad that he acts that way," Jill says with a look of disdain.

"Why does it make you mad? He's just being himself," Amber almost sounded like she was defending Andrew.

"Well, I don't know. Doesn't it bother you that he makes you feel uncomfortable in meetings?"

Amber answered, "I don't like feeling uncomfortable, but it's my issue that I don't like conflict. I try to focus on the facts of what we are talking about. If Andrew and Miriam don't get along, as long as it doesn't impact me getting my work done, it's not really my problem to fix."

Jill rubs her chin as she ponders what Amber is saying, then says with a smile, "You are just so much more patient than I am."

Amber smiles as their food comes and the conversation shifts to weekend plans.

Scenario Questions

1. Describe thoughts and/or actions in the scenario that you believe are driven by feelings rather than logical objectivity. Why do you think they are not driven by logical thinking?

    _____

    _____

    _____

2. Describe thoughts and/or actions in the scenario that indicate objective thinking. Why do you think they are driven by objective thinking?

    _____

    _____

    _____

3. Think of three key relationships you have right now. These could be with your spouse, a sibling, one of your children, a close friend or a co-worker. Think of the last three conversations you had with the person. Honestly assess whether you are being objective in your thinking about the relationship or not. If you are not, schedule a meeting with that person to get their

perspective. Create an action plan based on
that meeting to improve your thinking if
necessary. Use the table below to answer these
questions. Some examples are provided.

Relationship/Name	Conversation	Objective or Not? Why?
Mother-in-law	What to name the baby	Not, MIL is trying to manipulate us to name the baby after her mother. I get frustrated and don't want to talk to her. I haven't asked her why she thinks we should name the baby Mable.
George Edison, co-worker	George insists we have our weekly project meetings on Monday morning	Yes, he's explained, based on polling all team members, that Monday meetings help them re-engage in work after the weekend, and help them focus on what to achieve during the week and the week after.

REFLECTIVE QUESTIONS

- Based on what you learned about objective thinking, how do you need to change in the way you process information and interactions with your family, spouse, friends and co-workers?

_____

_____

_____

- Review the Chinese proverb below and reflect on how it can improve your thinking habits and process.

> *The men of old . . . first set up good government in their own states; wanting good government in their states, they first established order in their own families; wanting order in the home, they first disciplined themselves; desiring self-discipline, they rectified their own hearts; and wanting to rectify hearts, they sought precise verbal definitions of their inarticulate thoughts.*

_____

_____

_____

FOCUS AND PLAN

There's no better time than now to look at the path you have chosen for your relationship with God and with others to determine whether you are on the right path. You can do a better job of assessing and planning change using the Tools provided at the end of this book.

Focus

After you have completed the surveys at the end of this book you may see some areas that you want to change. Wanting to change is not the same thing as taking action to change. If you want something, especially if it will help you, but take no action, it will create tension in your life. You can either choose to stop wanting the change or take action to resolve the tension. Consider this definition of pain: *not accepting the reality of how it is*. You create pain in your life because you want reality to be different than it is. But reality is what it is. Accepting that leads to the important questions: where do you want to go from here, and what actions do you need to take to get there?

The change is either supported by God's Word, or not. It is either good or bad, righteous or unrighteous thinking. It is the truth, or an opinion, yours, or someone else's. If it is truth, supported by God's Word, then it makes sense to make the change. But your unrenewed mind is still driving your feelings, despite you knowing God's thinking is the best. Your old thinking and feelings will not support making the changes God desires. Remember this statement, "Just because you do right, doesn't mean you will feel right." Just because you do something that fits God's Word does not mean that your sin nature thinking and feelings will support you. That's why you invest in God's thinking and renew your mind to His ways. You can also think about it this way to engage your feelings; invest your feelings into pleasing God.

When you think about the difference between those times you made changes and the times you didn't, you may find an obstacle to change. You may think or say something like, "I can see how much damage my behavior creates in relationships, and I need to reflect on how to start acting differently. The problem is that I am too busy dealing with some unique and special challenges. The worst of it will be over in a few months. Then, when I can stop and breathe, I will make the changes I need to make."

That thinking is not reality. Busyness and difficulty are part of life. If a change benefits a relationship, you want the change, or you don't. You will likely act when you want something and clearly see the difference between that want and where you are. Robert Fritz calls that *structural tension*. And you tend to take time to do the things you want, right?

The real question is, "What am I willing to change *now?*"

Change requires discipline and focus. People who change focus on where they want to be and where they are, then they take one action at a time, even on behaviors that are difficult to change. If you have too many options, you may be overwhelmed, resulting in inaction. That is when you focus on one or two moves to get started, which increases the probability of change.

When you focus you put more energy into one or two things. Think of a water hose without a pressure nozzle. If you want to get the water to come out of the hose with greater intensity, you partially cover the opening at the end of the hose with your thumb. This creates a smaller opening and yields higher intensity and allows you to spray the water farther. Apply that principle to your life. Focus on a few things instead of trying to do everything. *Put your thumb over the end of the hose,* so your energy is intensified into one to three items.

Research provides some great insight. If people have accountability partners, they increase the odds that they will change. The American Society for Training and Development (now the Association for Talent Development, or ATD) studied what helps people implement information received during training. Listening and planning get you 50 percent of the way there, but involving others moves the probability of your success in your favor. Everyone needs accountability. Unfortunately, few people want it or seek it.

Action Taken	Probability of Implementing
Listen to an idea	10%
Consciously decide to adopt an idea	25%
Decide when to act on the idea	40%
Design a plan to act on the idea	50%
Commit to another person to act on the plan	65%
Get a specific accountability appointment with the person to whom you made your commitment	95%

Focus for Change

Identifying what needs to change is seldom as difficult as actually measuring change. Figure out a measurable result you want to achieve so that subjectivity does not take over. Find a metric that measures your progress and is specific enough for you to know if you achieved it or not. If someone else can read your metric for results and determine whether you are achieving it or not, that's a good indicator that you have clarity on the metric.

For example, a person thinks about their relationship, reviews the survey items, and decides that communication will be their focus. Communication is too broad a category, and not focused. Coach yourself. Ask these questions:

"How would I know if I am communicating?" Or, "If someone asked me every day if I was communicating, how could I be sure I could answer with a *yes*?"

Communication, like many other items, can be broken down into separate elements that allow clarity and focus on the sender, the receiver, and the time spent doing it. When you speak, is it clear? Are you listening? Are you spending time conversing? Even when separated into three elements, you may have the tendency to try to work on all three. That is not a focused approach. Take bite-size chunks to stay focused. Any of these three would work. For example:

Listening: "Ask at least 3 questions to aid my understanding of their point of view and summarize each conversation to be sure I understood."

Speaking: "Ask at least twice in each conversation if I am making sense, clear enough or being understood."

Time: "Spend at least 30 minutes, without distractions, sharing and listening, specifically to see life through their eyes."

Generally, for an issue like communication, focusing on the time element will create a structure to practice listening and speaking. While there are reasonable arguments to be made about *quality versus quantity* of time, err on the side of quantity, as time spent listening and asking questions provides a context for strong communication in a relationship.

Personal Plan

Thinking about your THERE, which you learned about earlier in this book. It's your desired destination. Then, you assess where you are now and what steps and actions you need to take to get from HERE to THERE. Knowing where you want to go is key to helping you get there. When you attach your values to your THERE, it gives you a stronger impetus to achieve what you are striving for.

Think about going from HERE to THERE in terms of traveling. If you were driving from one city to another in your state, you would probably not just jump in your car! You would figure out what time you needed to be in the other city, determine how long it would take you to get there, traffic you might face, so you can plan to get from here to there.

Establishing dates with any kind of plan gives you a target. Written deadlines are a huge motivator any time you are trying to get something accomplished. Thinking of making the change described earlier about changing how much time you spend conversing with someone each day, you must be honest about what the HERE is. If it's five minutes as you drink coffee each morning and you want to get to 30 minutes a day, you have a realistic view of what you need to change. To improve your odds of achieving your result, share it

THP Personal Planning Form

1. THERE—Goals, Desired Outcomes (Picturable, Measurable, Specific)		Due Date	
2. HERE—Current Reality			
3. PATH—Actions	**Progress Measures**	**Partners**	**Date**
Date Prepared:	Approved by:		

242 Spring Park Drive, Ste A   Midland, Texas 79705   Phone: 432-682-6823   https://gr8relate.com   Email: info.gr8relate@gr8grp.com

with an accountability partner who can help you stay on track.

Focus Triangle

The simplicity of this tool is what makes it so useful. You can use a blank sheet of paper or download the form. Both will work.

Focus Triangle

instructions

1. List items that you need to do in the **INTEND** section. Use the back for more.
2. Review the INTEND list and write 1 to 3 that you commit to do today in the **COMMIT** section.
3. Review the INTEND list and write up to 6 items you will ATTEMPT to do today.
4. All other items stay on your INTEND list to be reviewed tomorrow or in the near future.

COMMIT

ATTEMPT

INTEND

242 Spring Park Drive, Ste A   Midland, Texas 79705   Phone: 432-682-6823   https://gr8relate.com   Email: support@gr8relate.com

The bottom of the triangle is where you list all of the things you need, like, or INTEND to do today. The middle of the triangle is what you will ATTEMPT to do, and the top is what you will COMMIT to do.

The instructions are simple, and best done in this order.

1. List items you need to do in the INTEND section.

2. Review the INTEND list and write 1 to 3 that you commit to doing today in the COMMIT section. You can cross off or delete the items you selected from the INTEND list, if you want.

3. Review the INTEND list and write up to six items you will ATTEMPT to do today. You can cross off or delete those items in the INTEND list, also.

4. Leave all the remaining items in the INTEND section. If you are highly productive you can do some of those after you complete your COMMIT and ATTEMPT items.

The Focus Triangle form is available for download at this URL – https://gr8relate.com/wp-content/uploads/2022/06/Focus-Triangle-GR8R.pdf.

Identify Your Values

Values are evident in your thinking, feelings, and actions. In fact, values dictate where your resources of time and money are spent. Jesus puts it this way in Matthew:

> *Where your treasure is, there your heart will be also.*

Matthew 5:21, NKJV

Jesus was referring to money in that passage, stating that you will be focused on where your treasure is, thinking about it, feeling about it, and acting in line with it. You can apply that to the broader thought of values. What you value, therefore, must be clear and re-evaluated often.

Choosing values from a list can encourage you to intellectualize and fantasize about what you consider as important, and does not work as well as looking at your life to see the values you are living. When you look into the events of your life you can uncover the values you demonstrate in your day-to-day actions and interactions.

The following exercise helps develop your Values and a Purpose Slogan. It is not an easy exercise. I completed it in a couple of hours, then meditated on the values for months before I finalized my Purpose statement: "Pursuing the best for others through truth, faith, and integrity."

The following questions will help you reveal existing values. As you answer the questions, you will see values, but you may not have the right words. Words will matter in the long run, but in the short run, get an approximate label for the value. The questions can also be extremely helpful in learning more about yourself.

The wording will probably change, so use a pencil or use a computer. Getting it right the first time is not critical. Feel free to use the eraser and delete button liberally.

When creating your values list, it is okay to string value words together. Put a slash between the words that are similar in concept. For example, *Integrity/honesty/walk-the-talk* or *Integrity/whole/congruent*. After you create a string of words, determine which is the best description of the value and put it at the front of the string.

It may take several months to create a complete list of values. It is unlikely that you will capture them accurately and completely in one sitting. So, consider the first time as the beginning.

Clearly defined values create focus and direction for your choices, especially when facing crossroads.

Answer each question, preferably with one word or a short phrase. After you write your word or phrase, write *your* definition of the word or phrase. Capture how you see that word, rather than how others define it. Obviously, use a dictionary if needed.

1. Describe yourself in one word.	
Word/phrase	My description

2. Think of two important people in your life. List one word to describe each of those people.	
Word/phrase	My description
Word/phrase	My description

3. Name one of your traits you would like to pass on to a child.	
Word/phrase	My description

4. You just started your own country. On your money it says, "In _____ we trust."	
Word/phrase	My description

5. What are two qualities you look for in a life partner?	
Word/phrase	My description

Word/phrase	My description

6. Finish this quote by Gandhi and make it your own. "Whenever you are confronted with an opponent, conquer him with _____."

Word/phrase	My description

7. If there were just two rules everyone should follow, what would they be?

Word/phrase	My description

Word/phrase	My description

8. Think of a famous person you admire. In one word, why?

Word/phrase	My description

9. Voltaire said, "Ice cream is exquisite—what a pity it isn't illegal." What do you consider as exquisite in life?

Word/phrase	My description

For the following, write your answer then select the values from that answer. You can use a separate sheet for your answer if you want to provide more details.

10. Pick a moment in your life when life was especially rewarding or significant. Who was present? What was happening?	
Answer	
Word/phrase	My description
Word/phrase	My description

Word/phrase	My description

11. Pick a moment when you were very emotional and upset. Describe your emotions. Who was present? What was happening?

Answer

Word/phrase	My description

Word/phrase	My description

Word/phrase	My description

12. Determine what you must have in your life in order to be fulfilled. What are your must-haves? (For example: Must you have adventure and excitement, partnership and collaboration, a sense of accomplishment or success? Must you have or surround yourself with beauty or beautifult things? What form of creativity and self-expression must you have?)

Answer

Word/phrase	My description
Word/phrase	My description
Word/phrase	My description

13. We are capable of obsessive behavior, inflating it into a demand (ideal) rather than just a form of proper self-expression. What do people say about you? What do you say about yourself? What do people tease you about, or that drives them nuts? Write about a time when you had a case of *"my way or the highway."*

Answer	
Word/phrase	My description
Word/phrase	My description
Word/phrase	My description

Prioritize Your Values

With the list of values you are ready to determine which are the most important to you. The very definition of the word *values* means that what you have listed is important. Now identify the top priority values in your life.

First, review the list of values that you created and determine if you have any that should be combined. The definitions you used are the keys to knowing whether values should be combined.

Next, select no more than ten values from the list and write them on a table like the Top Ten Values table shown. There is no need to try to prioritize them as you write them on the table. The exercise will help you do that.

TOP TEN VALUES	TOP FIVE	TOP FOUR	TOP THREE	TOP TWO	#ONE
1					
2					
3					
4					
5					
6					
7					

8					
9					
10					

Complete each of the following steps and, if you are using the table, you will identify the values that are most important to you.

1. Imagine that you are only permitted to have five values on the list. Which ones would you give up? Put a check mark in the Top Five column for the 5 you are keeping. Cross off or draw a line through the five that you are giving up.

2. Now imagine you can only have four values. Which one would you give up? Cross it off and put check marks for the remaining four in the Top Four column.

3. Now cross off another and put check marks in the Top Three column to bring your list down to three

4. Now cross off another and make the check marks to bring your list to two

5. Finally, cross off one of your two remaining values. This is the one value on the list that you care about the most. Put in checkmark in the Top Value column.

This exercise can create some interesting reactions. It is not unusual to be frustrated as you are asked to choose between the values you have listed.

Reflect on what you were thinking or feeling when you gave up that last value. How did it feel to give up what you value? Have you ever had those thoughts or feelings before, at home or at work? Most likely those feelings have been there before because most people have, at one time or another, ignored or disregarded those things they value.

This exercise serves a dual purpose. It not only helps you identify your top values, but it also teaches a lesson about values.

When values are threatened, ignored, or disregarded, expect tension and stress to follow. If you do not honor what you deem important, it makes sense that something is not going to quite feel right. That is why it is important to identify critical values in your life. Without clearly defining them, you may not be able to identify the reason you are so unsettled. Defining your values and putting them in an easy-to-remember format helps you quickly assess when you are violating those things you hold dear.

Your Top Three Values

1. How would your life be different if those values were prominent and consistently

practiced? What evidence would you have
that your life was different?

_____

_____

_____

2. What would your family or organization look
    like if you consistently led people based on the
    values you have chosen?

_____

_____

_____

3. How does your current behavior *detract* from
    the values and vision you have for the family
    or organization you want in the future?

_____

_____

_____

Purpose / Mission

If you would like to take a shortcut approach to
developing a purpose statement, use your top three to
five values. Develop a short phrase or statement that
summarizes the values you identified.

Getting the statement into a form that you like may take some time but creating the first draft can be done rather quickly.

1. List your top three to five values.

_____

_____

_____

2. Think of how others could benefit from you living your values.

_____

_____

_____

3. Create a phrase that starts with how others will benefit from your values and then list your values.

_____

_____

_____

The second step in the process is crucial. When I first did this exercise many years ago, I did not have that second step, therefore, I created a phrase to remember my top three values of truth, faith, and integrity. Remembering those three words was not difficult, but something was missing. When I considered how my values could benefit others, and not just me, it helped me create a statement that is not only easy for me to remember but is a call to action for me. My purpose statement became, "Pursuing the best for others through truth, faith, and integrity."

Try it. The statement tends to work best when you put the benefit to others at the front.

If you want to do something more than use your values as a purpose statement, the following questions can be helpful. It will help to capture your answers on paper or electronically on a computer so you can reflect on them. Answering the questions is relatively easy. Developing them into a purpose statement can take more time. I would suggest that you take about an hour to think about the following questions and write your first draft.

1. What are three things you really want to accomplish in the next ten years?
2. Think about a time you were really excited about life. You were healthy, alive, together, and passionate. Describe what you were doing. Who was there? What was the situation?
3. Consider yourself on your current life journey. What is your journey about?
4. Think of the person that knows you best. What would he or she say are your strengths? List up to three.

5. Write how you could use those strengths to make a positive contribution—with your family, at work, and with friends.
6. If you could turn back the clock, what significant changes would you make?
7. What are you most proud of so far?
8. If you had $1,000,000 to give to a cause, what would it be and how would you advise them to use it?
9. What is the most important thing you can do in each of these areas that will have the most positive impact on your life—Physical, Mental, Social/Emotional, Spiritual?

Use that information to begin developing your purpose statement. The easiest first draft would simply be combining the answers. Then start revising so that it would make more sense. Obviously, combine similar thoughts and add elements to provide a richer meaning.

Here is a simple process to use as you develop your statement. Dr. Fred Lybrand has developed a writing course that suggests the following three guidelines to write anything.

☐ Write something—make it readable, not perfect, just workable.
☐ Get help—ask others to provide input on how to improve it.

☐ Make it better—make revisions from what others said and what you see as better.

Try it! Taking the time to define a purpose statement can be extremely rewarding. It can get you focused on what is most important to you.

STUDY GUIDE

Scripture Meditation

Time: 30 minutes a day

Each day read and meditate on one of the scriptures listed below, or as directed by your session leader.

Follow these steps.

1. Get in a quiet place without distraction.
2. Play a praise song, and just listen to the words.
3. Ask God to reveal His heart and meaning to you as you read the scriptures.
4. Write your reflections below or in your journal.
5. Read the scriptures daily so you receive maximum revelation.

Genesis 1:26-28, NKJV	Romans 6:13, NKJV	Romans 7:14-20, NKJV
Psalm 121:1-2, NKJV	Genesis 3:16-17, NKJV	Ephesians 5:25-31, NKJV
1 Timothy 2:14, NKJV	Genesis 2:15, NKJV	Genesis 2:5, NKJV
Romans 6:16, NKJV	John 15:10, NKJV	Jeremiah 17:9, NKJV
Proverbs 3:5-6, NKJV	Matthew 5:21, NKJV	Habakkuk 2:2, NKJV

REFLECTIVE QUESTIONS

- Thinking about your life over the last 5-10 years. Have you chosen a path that focuses on only you, or have you been focused on glorifying God?

_____

_____

_____

_____

- If you have not been focused on glorifying God, what specific problems has that caused you? What were the ultimate consequences you experienced in those instances?

_____

_____

_____

_____

- Think about how God designed you versus the _Unknown Judgments_, how specifically has that played out in your life? For example, if you are a man, you work hard and want to provide, but you find yourself getting frustrated with how

hard you work and it seems you can't *get ahead.*
For a woman, maybe you love your children
dearly, but find lots of struggles with raising
them during their teenage years.

_____

_____

_____

_____

- What challenges do you have with changing
  behavior? How can you change your mindset to
  better deal with change?

_____

_____

_____

_____

- What is your purpose and mission in life? How
  does that relate to your relationship with God?

_____

_____

_____

_____

TOOLS

Each book in this series has a supplemental video course on www.gr8relate.com/video-courses/ under the heading "BOOK SERIES Video Courses." The videos were selected from the COMPLETE Video Courses to support the book and provide more details. If you want more details than the book offers, use the COMPLETE Video Courses and the GR8 Relationships Study Guide.

The following tools will enable you to understand yourself and your spouse and how you can work together to handle conflict. The videos listed below are a part of the video course that corresponds to the information in this book. Completing all the courses will be instrumental in helping you find FREEDOM!

You can find all these tools and many more on our website, www.gr8relate.com, on the TOOLS tab.

Kolbe Assessment https://gr8relate.com/kolbe

You can trust the validity and accuracy of the Kolbe instrument to show you your strengths and instincts. The Kolbe also helps you easily see and understand how the strengths and talents of one person may not be considered as strengths by another. This critical information will help you bridge the gap between reality and your expectations of them. Once you complete the assessment, you will receive detailed reports that will help you understand your strengths and talents and how to use your strengths in a complementary way with your spouse, family member, or friend's strengths. By understanding your instincts, you can more easily discuss your differences, laugh about them and develop ways to deal with them.

The Thomas-Kilman Conflict Mode Instrument (TKI) https://gr8relate.com/tki

The TKI is the world's best-selling instrument for understanding conflict. It helps you see that conflict can be beneficial and useful instead of thinking conflict as bad. You will be provided detailed information on effectively using all five conflict modes—competing, collaborating, compromising, avoiding, and accommodating.

The Fundamental Interpersonal Relations Orientation-Behavior™ (FIRO-B®). https://gr8relate.com/firob

The FIRO-B helps you understand how you interact at work and personal life. This easy-to-complete assessment will provide critical insights into how an individual interacts with others. This personality instrument measures how you typically behave with others and how you expect them to act toward you.

Individual Videos

We have a FREE video course that corresponds with the information in this book.

These are short courses that you can watch/listen at your own pace. Enter the information in parenthesis below into your browser and you will be taken to a video course. When you are online, scroll down and click the "Sign Up / Start Course" button to create an account. You only need an account to access all the free courses.

There are two options:

- BOOK SERIES Courses: Each book in the GR8 Relationships series will have a video course with specific videos selected from the COMPLETE Courses that help explain the contents of the book. This book's video course is below.
    - Did You Choose the Right Path? (https://gr8relate.com/video-courses/did-you-choose-the-right-path/)
- COMPLETE Courses: These are the original, complete courses that give you

more details about the information in this book.

- 01 – Overview and Personal Assessment (https://gr8relate.com/video-courses/overview-and-personal-assessment/)
- 04A - The Unknown Judgment for Women (https://gr8relate.com/video-courses/unknown-judgment-for-women/)
- 04B - The Unknown Judgment for Men (https://gr8relate.com/video-courses/unknown-judgment-for-men/)
- 04C – The PROBLEM Started in the Garden (https://gr8relate.com/video-courses/battle-between-designs-and-judgments/)

Ten Steps to Your Best Relationships!

Do you desire to have better, healthier relationships? Do you find that on some days, it seems like a struggle? If so, you are not alone. Here are ten steps that can lead you to experience your best relationships ever.

Step 1. Study God's Design for Excellent Relationships

The design of a butter knife lets you know that it works best when spreading soft things like room-temperature butter. If you try to use it to cut a T-bone steak, you will see that it is not designed to do that. The same is true for excellent relationships.

God had a clear purpose and design when He created man and woman. He designed man to be different from a woman so that the two would not only be complimentary but, more importantly, display His image to a lost and dying world.

Step 2. Recognize How Men and Women Are Different - REALLY!

God created man and woman perfectly to fulfill their designed roles which complement each other.

If you remember, God created Eve because He did not want Adam alone. Without a woman, man has no one to help "fill the earth and subdue it" (Gen 1:28). Adam needed a suitable helper to fulfill God's purpose for mankind. And for a woman, it is imperative to remember that Helper is a word used primarily about God (i.e., Ps 121:1-2), further elevating rather than demeaning women.

God designed a woman to fulfill a relational role while a man fulfills his work role design – the differences are complementary, not conflicting.

Step 3. Accept the ONE PROBLEM!

Did you know that there is only ONE PROBLEM?

Making everything about ME is THE PROBLEM that destroys relationships. It is the root from which relationship mistakes grow. Unfortunately, we are blind to how often we make life about ME! You may have noticed how easy it is to see when others are being selfish and self-absorbed, but not when you are doing it.

When others are making life about ME, it's like they have this big ME on their forehead. They cannot see it – because it is on their forehead above their eyes! The same is true for you; they see it!

Step 4. Discover the Unknown Judgments for Men and Women

Every woman and man that has, is, and will live is subject to the judgments issued by God. And this affects every relationship.

Understanding these judgments is like unlocking the secrets of what drives and motivates lousy relationships. Learning these profound judgments enables you to identify difficulties and issues in your relationships and see the damage they are creating for you now.

Woman

- **Designed to RELATE:** The woman's unique design helps, nurtures, and supports healthy relationships, especially with her husband and children.
- **RELATING is Judged:** The woman's judgment adds pain to relationships and drives her to control them, which creates more pain, especially with her husband and children.

Pursuing their BEST

THP Personal Planning Form

1. **THERE**—Goals, Desired Outcomes (Picturable, Measurable, Specific)	**Due Date**	

2. **HERE**—Current Reality	

3. **PATH**—Actions	**Progress Measures**	**Partners**	**Date**
Date Prepared:	Approved by:		

242 Spring Park Drive, Ste A   Midland, Texas 79705   Phone: 432-682-6823   https://gr8relate.com   Email: info.gr8relate@gr8grp.com

Focus Triangle

Instructions

1. List items that you need to do in the **INTEND** section. Use the back for more.
2. Review the INTEND list and write 1 to 3 that you commit to do today in the **COMMIT** section.
3. Review the INTEND list and write up to 6 items you will ATTEMPT to do today.
4. All other items stay on your INTEND list to be reviewed tomorrow or in the near future.

COMMIT

ATTEMPT

INTEND

Two Ways to Live

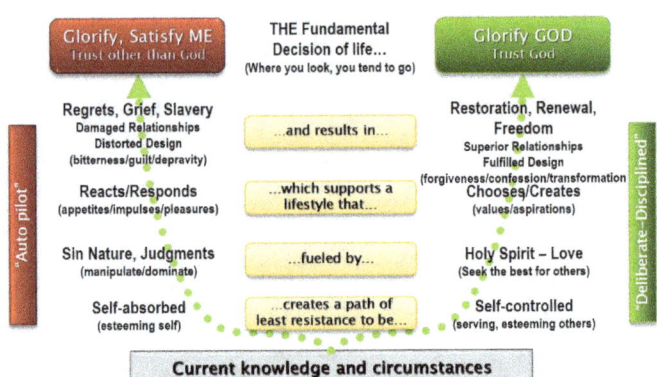

Current knowledge and circumstances

You are designed in the image of God. You only need to depend upon God to allow your design to reflect the image of God. The natural tendency, though, is to rely upon yourself, which will hide or distort your design. It is automatic (Auto Pilot) to depend on and trust YOURSELF, which follows the Self-absorbed and Judgment path. It requires a Deliberate choice to trust God.

When you look at your current reality, some things are known, and others aren't. Part of your current reality is that you either know what God is asking you to do in this current circumstance or don't. You either know God's Word, or you don't. God's Word is all about reality and how things work. If you did an objective report on your life right now, that would be a good picture of your **Current knowledge and circumstances** or, as you have learned, your current reality. Right now, you are standing in the current knowledge and circumstances rectangle.

As you stand in current reality, you have two choices or places to look. Remember, "Where you look, you tend to go?" God asks you where you are looking when He asks The Fundamental Question, "Do you trust God or something other than God?" God continually asks you that one question. It comes in two critical forms, one for eternal life ("Do you trust Me for your eternity?") and one for daily life ("Do you trust Me now?"). If you accepted God's gift of Salvation and eternal life with Him, He asks you the second question. If you haven't, you get the first and often the second question to drive you back to the first one. Everyone faces these two questions. If you are blind to them, then you are depending on yourself, not God. Looking at God and trusting Him provides the best results.

If you look at, **Satisfy ME** or *Trust other than God*, you create a path of least resistance to being self-absorbed and self-dependent. That is the natural tendency of the sin nature to esteem yourself rather than others. When temptation comes, there is a greater chance to sin because of your self-absorbed, satisfy ME attitude. You will be less willing to endure short-term pain; therefore, there will be long-term pain from the regrets of your self-absorbed actions. On the other hand, if you look at **Glorify and Trust**

ENDNOTES

1   Biblical Theology of the Old Testament, Roy Zuck,
    et al. Moody Publishers, 1991, pp. 13, 14.
2   Henry, M. (1994). Matthew Henry's commentary
    on the whole Bible: complete and unabridged in one
    volume (p. 14). Hendrickson.